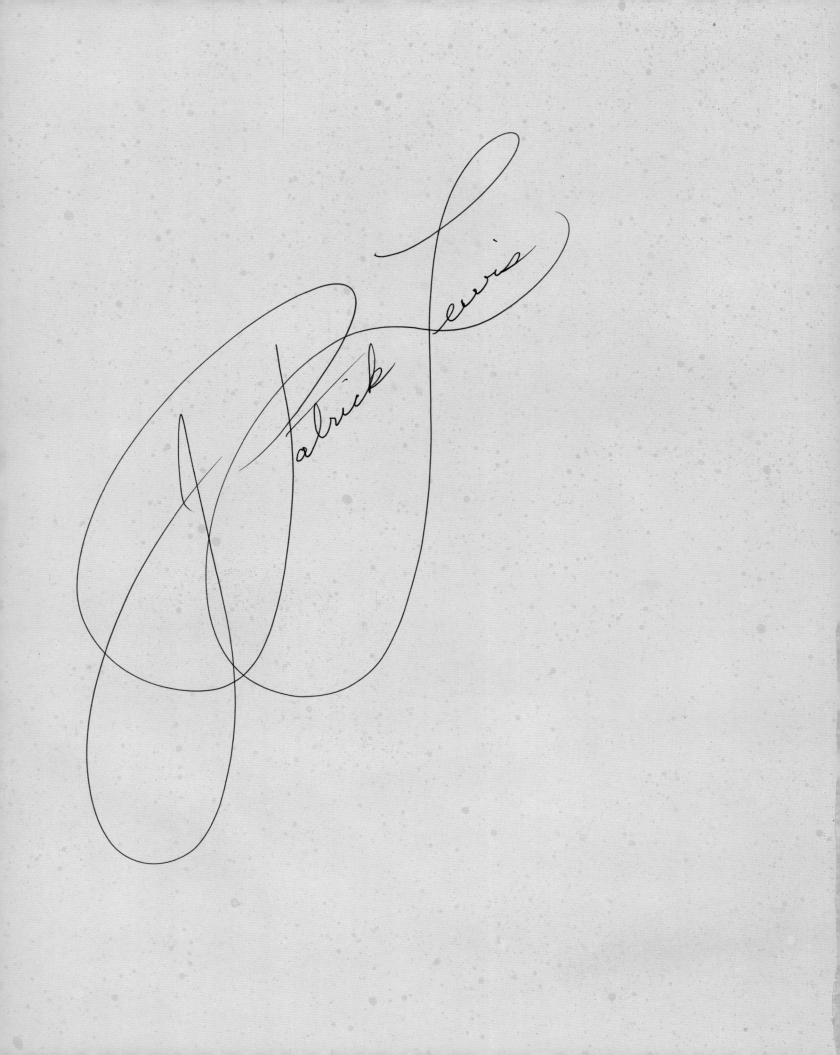

EARTH & YOU
A CLOSER VIEW

NATURE'S FEATURES

**THE FIRST OF THREE BOOKS
CELEBRATING THE HUMAN CONNECTION WITH
NATURE'S FEATURES,
NATURE'S CREATURES,
AND NATURE'S PAST AND FUTURE**

BY J. PATRICK LEWIS • ILLUSTRATIONS BY CHRISTOPHER CANYON

DAWN PUBLICATIONS

DEDICATIONS

For Kyriacos and Diane — JPL

To the teachers of the Program for Young Children at the Columbus School for Girls for all of the joy, wonder, knowledge, creativity, wisdom and love that you give and share everyday. — CC

Copyright © 2000 J. Patrick Lewis
Illustrations copyright © 2000 Christopher Canyon

A Sharing Nature With Children Book

Library of Congress Cataloging-in-Publication Data

Lewis, J. Patrick.
   Earth and you-a closer view : nature's features / by J. Patrick Lewis ; illustrated by Christopher Canyon.— 1st ed.
     p. cm. — (A sharing nature with children book)
   ISBN 1-58469-015-1 (pbk.) — ISBN 1-58469-016-X (hardback)
   1. Nature—Juvenile literature. 2. Physical geography—Juvenile literature. [1. Nature. 2. Physical geography. 3. Ecology.] I. Canyon,
Christopher, ill. II. Title. III. Series.
  QH48 .L48 2001
  508—dc21

                      00-011499

Dawn Publications
P.O. Box 2010
Nevada City, CA 95959
530-478-0111
nature@dawnpub.com
www.dawnpub.com

Published in Japan by Mikuni Publishing, Tokyo.
Printed in Hong Kong

10 9 8 7 6 5 4 3 2 1
First Edition

Design and computer production by Andrea Miles

The Earth is in you, the Earth is in me,
The Earth is in every flower and tree,
On the silent land, in the raging sea,
In animals and humanity.

EARTH

Imagine sitting on the
   bright side of the Moon.
What does the Earth look like from there?
At first you may not recognize
   that distant dome.
Until you realize . . . it's home.

Make the Earth your companion.
   Walk lightly on it,
   as other creatures do.

And the Earth is rinsed by the . . .

SKY

Look up there!
Clouds tattoo the dazzling blue heavens.
  After a thundershower, Sky and Sun write
  their names . . .

Wherever you go, whatever you do,
  the Sky is always watching over you.

And the Sky is the ceiling of the . . .

SEA

Seagulls turn the wind.
Wind plows the waves.
Waves stroke the shore.
Shore keeps the shell.

Can you find a conch?
  Hold it up to your ear
  and hear the wind in the waves
  on the shore in the shell.

Let the Sea be horizon to hope,
  let seashore be the landfall
  you dream on.

And the Sea curls its arm into a . . .

RIVER

Listen to the rush of white water.
  Listen to the hush of blue water.
   And watch it move as it moves you.
Have you ever heard anything so soothing
  on a summer's day as a river trickling
  along without a care?

Let the rhythm of the River carry
  worry away—and remind you that
  everything will pass.

And the River cups its hand into a . . .

LAKE

See the fishes at play,
See the seaweed swaying,
See the turtle paddling away.
You are looking down into a lake—
one of nature's own windowpanes.

Like the Lake,
  know when to be rough,
  when to reflect,
  when to be clear and calm.

And the Lake is a mirror to the . . .

MOUNTAIN

Visit a mountain for courage.
Look at a mountain in awe.
Climb a mountain for strength.
Stand on a mountain, and you might
  think for a little while that you can
  fly as far as forever.

Always remember that a mountain
  isn't waiting to be conquered.
Like you, the mountain is waiting
  for a friend.

And the Mountain is sister to the . . .

VOLCANO

is a mountain that fountains fire from its
hot rock belly. Burning lava rolls all the
way to the sea where it dangles from
cliffs like ribbons of orange candy. . .

Or suddenly, from under the sea itself, a
volcanic surprise—a gleaming, steaming
new island. Otherwise, it sleeps for
centuries.

Like Volcanoes, whose magma boils
beneath the Earth's surface, hold your
temper. Be slow to anger, quick to cool.

And the Volcano towers above the . . .

WOODLAND

In winter the skeleton elms click their ice songs;
In spring the maples wear haloes of birds;
In summer the oaks feed the squirrels;
In fall the colors feed your eyes.

The truest way to welcome wonder is to
   learn the name of
      each tree—elm, birch, beech;
      each bird—cardinal, jay, junco;
      each color—azure, cinnamon, holly.

Let the Woodland bring whispers to the wild,
   berries to the branches,
   nectar to the needy.

And the Woodland is cousin to the . . .

RAINFOREST

These giant trees are nature's umbrellas.
 Drip, drip, drip.
The sun pours its gold through millions of
 leaves, tigering the light.
A dense neighborhood of vines welcomes
 untold numbers of creatures,
 many as yet unnamed.

The Rainforest is Earth's garden,
 yet needs no gardener.
Left to itself, this butterfly kingdom
 is its own best keeper.

Let the green kingdom show us the
 nature of wisdom—
let the richest garden on Earth prove to
 us the wisdom of Nature.

And the Rainforest goes green to the . . .

WETLANDS

Rivers of grass, rich and wild, black ponds
and brown waters, rotting trees, and
feasts of mosquitoes. It's home to
everyone—birds resting from flight,
frogs announcing night,
and bugs in untold numbers.

Nowhere on Earth can you see more clearly
the renewal of life from its decay, where
vines of growth and signs of loss entwine.

Like the wetlands, welcome strangers.
You never know when
you might be a stranger, too.

And the Wetlands dry up to the . . .

GRASSLAND

Set your alarm clock early one morning to
   watch a broom of light sweep across a
   prairie, when sunrise has two minutes left
   to live. The picture will keep forever in
   the corners of your mind.

If you are very lucky, buffalo will oblige
   and dot the landscape like brown stars
   in yellow grass sky.

Imagine yourself in the middle of an
   endless prairie.
Would you stop and stand?
   Lie down and cloud-dream?
Would you turn and run?
   In which direction?
Ask the sun.

And the Grassland bounds softly towards the . . .

ICE LAND

The Palace of Whiteness rages blue,
  here where snow is emperor
  and ice is king.
On the drop edge of a dark bay,
  great walls of ice rip open
  the roaring sea.

What an orchestra of whales, walruses
  and seals!
When summer breaks, the cold will still be
  warm enough for swarming seabirds, and
  all you can do is stand and stare.

Is there a lesson here? Who knows?
  With fur-fat parkas and
  inch-thick boots, let's stay for the
  penguin party.

And the Ice Land is stranger to the

HOT LAND

Dry skies are orange by day, purple by night.
The desert likes to be alone.
When the rains come, it's a holiday for flowers.
Oh, the desert may be empty of people
  but it is still full of quiet fun!
Is it lonely here? Ask the lizard.
  She will turn her head sideways, which means No.

Let the Hot Land be home to stillness
  and wonder—and it will take your breath away!

And the Hot Land breezes up to the . . .

TOWN

At the end of the long frontier hums a hive
  called a community, where people like
  you and me nest and rest.
Towns as tiny as stop signs survive;
  cities as large as small countries thrive.

But what is any town
  without Earth's bounty?
No matter where you live,
  your world is a neighborhood that
  every living thing must share.

Let the town weave
  a small basket of togetherness.

And the Town is the keeper of the . . .

SCHOOL

Wherever you are, and faraway, there are
thousands of classrooms like this one
across the world.
All colors of children and teachers are at
work and play asking questions,
finding answers, solving mysteries,
and discovering if and what
and why and how.

Let the School teach you many things,
but never forget the One Thing:
Make the Earth your companion.
Walk lightly on it,
        as other creatures do.

And the School is a seed in the . . .

EARTH

The Earth is our home, but we do not own it.
The Earth is our garden, plant a flower, plant a tree.
The Earth is a gift, given only once.
The Earth is a friend. Keep her in your care.

The Earth is in you, the Earth is in me,
The Earth is in every flower and tree,
On the silent land, in the raging sea,
In animals and humanity.

For 30 years J. Patrick Lewis was a college profes-
sor, teaching economics. Now he plays with words and
hangs out with kids at elementary schools. He is out to
prove that "poetry is ear candy," and to inspire a sim-
patico connection with the natural wonders that sur-
round us. "If there is a better way to spend a lifetime,"
he says, "I can't imagine what it would be." This is his
first book with Dawn Publications.

Christopher Canyon is irrepressibly playful as well as
passionate about illustrating children's picture books.
He teaches illustration at the Columbus College of Art
& Design in Columbus, Ohio, is a frequent speaker at
professional events, and his illustrations have been
displayed in several national exhibitions. But his
favorite audience is children and he makes a point of
visiting schools often. Two of his previous books for
Dawn Publications, The Tree in the Ancient Forest and
Stickeen: John Muir and the Brave Little Dog, won the Benjamin Franklin
Award as best illustrated children's books of the year.

OTHER BOOKS ILLUSTRATED BY CHRISTOPHER CANYON

The Tree in the Ancient Forest, by Carol Reed-Jones. The plants and animals around a grand old fir are remarkably and wonderfully dependent upon each other. Christopher's magical realism, and Carol's cumulative verse serve both to inform the mind and inspire the soul.

Stickeen: John Muir and the Brave Little Dog by John Muir as retold by Donnell Rubay. In this classic true story, the relationship between the great naturalist and a small dog is changed forever by their adventure on a glacier in Alaska.

Wonderful Nature, Wonderful You, by Karin Ireland, shows how nature is a great teacher, reminding us to bloom where we are planted. This popular book celebrates nature's diversity and strong character traits—and with a light touch, suggests how humans can follow nature's example and make good choices.

A SAMPLING OF NATURE AWARENESS BOOKS FROM DAWN PUBLICATIONS

John Muir: My Life with Nature, by Joseph Cornell. John Muir's remarkable adventures and attunement with nature are told in his own words, written for a young audience by the author of the classic *Sharing Nature with Children.*

Girls Who Looked Under Rocks: The Lives of Six Pioneering Naturalists, by Jeannine Atkins. Six girls, from the 17th to the 20th century, didn't run from spiders or snakes but crouched down to take a closer look. They became pioneering naturalists.

Do Animals Have Feelings, Too?, by David Rice presents fascinating true stories of animal behavior, and then asks the reader whether they think the animal is acting on the basis of feelings or just instinctively.

Animal Acrostics, by David M. Hummon. Acrostic poems are a wonderful way to encourage children to write creatively. These "vertical poems" are amusing, clever, and informative.

This is the Sea that Feeds Us, by Robert F. Baldwin. In simple cumulative verse, beginning with tiny plankton, "floating free," this book explores the oceans' fabulous food chain that reaches all the way to whales and humans in an intricate web.

Salamander Rain, A Lake and Pond Journal by Krstin Joy Pratt. This young author-illustrator's fourth book is a "planet scout's" pond and lake journal—a subject known to be wet and muddy, but fun! Kristin is the teenage "eco-star" made famous by her books *A Walk in the Rainforest, A Swim through the Sea,* and *A Fly in the Sky.*

Dawn Publications is dedicated to inspiring in children a deeper understanding and appreciation for all life on Earth. To order, or for a copy of our catalog, please call 800-545-7475. You may also order, view the catalog, see reviews and much more online at www.dawnpub.com.